Other Books in

MW01520459

The Miracle of Self-Realization: Reflections on the Spiritual Teachings of Ramana Maharshi by Jeff Carreira

The Spiritual Implications of Quantum Physics: Reflections on the Nature of Science, Reality and Paradigm Shifts by Jeff Carreira

The Miracle of an Open Mind: Reflections on the Philosophy of William James by Jeff Carreira

Inner Peace in a Busy World: Reflections on Meditation and the Journey from Anxiety to Spiritual Freedom by Jeff Carreira

Evolution, Intuition and Reincarnation: Reflections on the spiritual vision of Ralph Waldo Emerson by Jeff Carreira

The Battle of Science and Spirituality: Reflections on the History of Western Philosophy by Jeff Carreira

Free Resources from Jeff Carreira

Life Without Fear: Meditation as an Antidote to Anxiety with Jeff Carreira. Visit lifewithoutfear.online

Secrets of Profound Meditation: Six Spiritual Insights that will Transform Your Life with Jeff Carreira. Visit secretsofprofoundmeditation.com

Foundations of a New Paradigm: A 6-part program designed to shift the way you experience everything with Jeff Carreira. Visit foundationsofanewparadigm.com

THE POWER OF
CREATIVE FLOW

REFLECTIONS ON PEAK PERFORMANCE, CULTURAL TRANSFORMATION, AND SPIRITUAL GROWTH

ISBN: 978-1-954642-40-9

Emergence Education
P.O. Box 63767
Philadelphia, PA 19147
EmergenceEducation.com

Cover design by Silvia Rodrigues.
Interior design by Sophie Peirce.

Printed in the United States of America.

THE POWER *of* CREATIVE FLOW

Reflections on
PEAK PERFORMANCE,
CULTURAL TRANSFORMATION,
AND SPIRITUAL GROWTH

JEFF CARREIRA

EMERGENCE EDUCATION
Philadelphia, Pennsylvania

Contents

The only way to make sense out of change is to plunge into it, move with it, and join the dance.

~ ALAN WATTS

The Path to Happiness and Enhanced Peak Performance

"Our limits are governed by flow's ability to amplify performance as much as by imagination's ability to dream up that performance."

– STEVEN KOTLER

I FIRST READ THE bestselling book *Flow* in the mid-1980's, about a decade after it was published in 1975. The author was the Hungarian-American psychologist Mihaly Csikszentmihalyi. The book introduced me to a miraculous state of consciousness that can unify our mental and physical faculties into perfect harmony. This extraordinary state of consciousness gives rise to a deep sense of interconnectedness with our surroundings and leads to an efficiency of action that produces peak performance and true happiness.

What could be more exciting? Before we dive into the extraordinary state of flow as Csikszentmihalyi explained it, I first want to introduce you to some of what I see as the origins of the idea in the writings of Ralph Waldo Emerson, the American transcendentalist of the 1840s and 50s. As this book unfolds, you will see that some of Emerson's ideas and those of many others that were influenced by him are closely associated with flow states.

Emerson is recognized as one of the primary

architects of a uniquely American cultural tradition called American Transcendentalism, or sometimes Concord Transcendentalism. For him, the distinction between the ideas of intuition and understanding was crucially important. Understanding is the knowing that comes from rational and logical thinking. Intuition is a burst of immediately recognized truth that comes to us spontaneously out of nowhere. Emerson was a towering figure of American Romanticism and as we will see in this book, he implanted the idea of intuition, or spontaneous knowing, deep in the American psyche where it would emerge to the surface at moments of cultural change again and again.

Emerson was an essayist and a public intellectual, but he was also a mystic and a spiritual teacher to many. One of the principal tenets of his mystical philosophy was the idea of Self-Reliance and he was not referring to a reliance upon our personality or ego. Emerson saw that we all have an individual mind, but we are also all connected to what he called the Oversoul, which he envisioned as a higher mind or the collective soul of all of humanity. Our intuitions, those spontaneous gems of undeniable certainty that appear to us out of nowhere, come from the Oversoul; they come from a global source. Emerson taught that we can all tap into that source of spontaneous wisdom far beyond the limitations of our individual separate minds.

When pursuing the power of intuition and

spontaneous wisdom, there are two questions that we will naturally want to address. The first is, how do we gain access to that mysterious flow of insight? And the second is, where does the wisdom of that flow come from? The first question is the more pragmatic of the two, the second, more esoteric, but both have been asked and answered many times throughout the ages. These same questions can be found in the philosophy of many cultures, but the scope of this little book will keep us predominantly, but not exclusively, focused on some of its American manifestations.

The Age of Reason, or the European Enlightenment, was an explosive time of cultural change that gave birth to our modern understanding of rational thinking. The significance of discovering this type of rational thinking is impossible to assess. In fact, it is probably impossible for us to fully appreciate how magnificent a breakthrough it really was. Can you imagine a time when people didn't realize that they had the capacity to think and figure things out? Instead, they assumed that God was the only one capable of knowing anything and therefore, anything they knew must come directly from him. Now of course, if you didn't believe you had any rational faculties, you wouldn't try to develop any. The Age of Reason was born out of a gradual recognition that there are logical principles that can be used to allow us to think clearly and figure things out. Western culture went from a time dominated by superstitious beliefs to the technological marvels and advancements that we enjoy today. The form of deductive rationality that was engineered during The Enlightenment was the way of knowing that Emerson called understanding, and that he wanted to contrast with another way of knowing called intuition.

The central project of the Enlightenment was the birth and development of the rational mind, or we could say understanding. By the middle of the 18th century, the wonders of rationality and science had proven so successful that many believed it would only be a matter of a few more decades before everything in the universe was known and understood. However, this unbridled enthusiasm for progress was soon shunted by two things. One was the living conditions of the Industrial Revolution that had begun to look as if it had made human life dramatically worse rather than better. The second stumbling block was the French Revolution. The precious ideals of the Enlightenment, which had given rise to the first modern democracy in America, had ignited a murderous mob when applied just a few years later in France. With blood running through the streets of Paris, many intellectuals, poets, and artists began to wonder if the Age of Reason had gone terribly wrong. In the wake of these perceived failures of rationality, the Romantic movement was born, and the power of intuition began to find new proponents.

As we have already stated, Ralph Waldo Emerson

was the leading figure of the Romantic movement known as American or Concord Transcendentalism, and Emerson's godson, William James, took some of that Romantic spirit with him into the next generation. As a young man, James, who would later become a famous psychologist and philosopher, was passionate about the possibility of accessing depths of mind beyond conscious awareness. He used automatic writing and the inhalation of nitrous oxide as a means of accessing the deeper layers of self that were hidden beneath the conscious layers of our psyche. During the years that he taught psychology at Harvard university, he set up America's first psychology laboratory and automatic writing was one of the things that he encouraged his students to experiment with.

One of his students, Gertrude Stein, would later take her experiences with automatic writing to Paris. During the early decades of the 20th century, Stein would become a central figure in the avant-garde movement there. Stein gained fame as a collector of extraordinary modern art created by as yet undiscovered geniuses such as Henri Matisse and Pablo Picasso. She, herself, was an experimental writer who explored the creative possibilities of writing spontaneously. She was a respected confidant and critic of a number of authors who would later become famous such as Ernest Hemingway, F. Scott Fitzgerald, and James Joyce. In the next chapter, we will take a detailed look at how the Romantic notion of accessing our hidden inner depths through spontaneous creation sparked yet another artistic revolution, this time in and around New York City in the middle of the 20th century.

There is one final historical development that I want to mention briefly so that the stage is completely set for our exploration of the phenomenon of flow states, and that is the growth of humanistic psychology.

Sometimes known as the third force, humanistic psychology was developed as a third approach to psychology different from the psychology of behaviorism on one hand, and Freudian psychoanalysis on the other. The psychological model of behaviorism saw all human behavior as the result of outside reinforcement. To behaviorists like B. F. Skinner, there was no reason to even try to understand the inner workings of the mind. The only thing that a scientifically inclined psychologist needed to be concerned with was the system of rewards and punishments offered by the patient's environment. Freud, on the other hand, saw the main job of the psychologist to be the excavation of the unconscious mind in search of the hidden urges and drivers that were the ultimate source of human behavior.

The new strain of humanistic psychology shifted the concerns of the profession toward the possibility of self-actualization. One of the most well-known humanistic psychologists was Abraham Maslow. His famous hierarchy of needs placed self-actualization as the pinnacle of human achievement. Central to Maslow's understanding of self-actualization were occurrences of peak experience which he recognized as a source of extreme joy and defined as *rare, exciting, oceanic, deeply moving, exhilarating, elevating experiences that generate an advanced form of perceiving reality, and are even mystic and magical in their effect upon the experimenter.*

In his bestselling book *Flow*, Mihaly Csikszentmihalyi offers a detailed study of the kinds of peak experiences that Maslow had also been preoccupied with and, like Maslow, Csikszentmihalyi was captivated by the dramatically positive effects they have on our experience of life as both an enhancer of performance and a source of happiness.

Csikszentmihalyi found that the experience of flow is characterized by five components that are all simultaneously present in that extraordinary state. I would like to describe these components here from my own experience of them.

1. In flow states, I feel intensely concentrated in an easeful, effortless way, with all of my attention intensely focused on the present moment.
2. The distinction between seeing and doing disappears and each action appears as a spontaneous unpremeditated response to the present moment.
3. There is an exhilarating sense of forgetting

myself and any sense of self-concern, which creates a sense of extreme happiness.

4. This amazing state of surrendered engagement paradoxically leads to a heightened sense of power and control.

5. And finally, whatever I am doing is rewarding in and of itself. I am not doing it for an outcome, but only because I love it.

Everyone has experienced this sense of flow in some circumstance or another. For one person it might be playing tennis or golf, for another, time spent in nature might induce a peak experience. Others may experience it by reading a book, or talking with friends, or cooking.

The activities that offer us the chance to be in flow are the things we would do all the time if we could, because they make us the happiest. In fact, from one point of view, most of our lives are spent in an effort to provide us with opportunities to be in flow. Csikszentmihalyi realized this and it inspired him to do the research that led to writing *Flow*. He hoped that the book would educate people about how flow states make us happy and how we can learn to enter them at will.

Happiness, however, is only one of the benefits of flow because these peak experiences also unleash our creative potential and enhance our ability to act in seemingly miraculous ways. Csikszentmihalyi's book was largely focused on the happiness that can be found through flow, but Steven Kotler's book, *The Rise of Superman*, explores the enhanced human performance unleashed in flow states. I would assert that when you see any magnificent human achievement, it was almost certainly attained by someone, or some group of people, in flow. Flow makes us happy, but it also leads to peak performance in just about anything. *The Rise of Superman* is a thrilling and exciting book that explores the flow states that carry athletes to excellence in extreme sports.

One story that is told in the book is the story of how Laird Hamilton famously surfed the monster wave at Teahupo'o. Hamilton was shuttled out in a jet ski, and as he began to approach the wave, everyone from the beach shouted for him to turn back because it was obvious that the wave was simply too big to ride. Hamilton went anyway.

The wave was massive and moving with such power that it threatened to pull him up and slam him back down onto the water's surface with extreme force. Hamilton survived because he instinctively dragged his hand in the water to hold himself down. This is now a standard practice of big wave surfing, but no one had ever ridden a wave that big before so there was no way for Hamilton to know to do that beforehand. The life-saving insight to drag his hand behind him came spontaneously from the heightened sensitivity of the flow state.

Hamilton, and many of the other extreme sports athletes profiled in Kotler's book, describe their experiences of flow. These states of intense yet wide-open focus allow them to achieve seemingly impossible feats. The stories I read in *The Rise of Superman* reminded me of a story I had read years earlier in a book called *Young Men and Fire* by Norman Maclean. That book recounts the story of the infamous forest fire that blew up at Mann Gulch in Montana in 1949. Fifteen fire jumpers parachuted in to fight that fire, but when the fire blew up in high winds all but three were overrun by flames and killed.

When the fire got out of control, the fire jumpers ran for the safety of a ridge. It soon became clear that they would not make it to safety in time. Under the pressure of impending doom, the foreman of the group, Wag Dodge, had a flash of insight. He lit a fire around him that he could hide in as the larger fire burned around it. He shouted for the others to join him in the center of the burned-out area he had created. No one joined him, instead they ran for the ridge and all but two perished. Dodge survived in his fire pit.

Wag Dodge, under the pressure of certain death, had invented what has come to be known as an escape fire. Firefighters are now trained to start fires that will burn off all of the fuel ahead of a larger fire and then lay in it as the larger fire blows over them. How did Dodge know to do this? I can only imagine that, like Hamilton, he had tapped into a higher source of insight that became available in a flow state that connected him with the spontaneous wisdom that arises in response to the present moment.

The question that fascinates me is, where does this spontaneous wisdom come from? It isn't produced by logical reasoning; it simply appears, faster than thought would allow, at exactly the moment it is needed. When this kind of intuition arises, we don't know where it comes from. In the two cases I just described, it was coming in the midst of completely novel circumstances in which there was no specific previous experience for either Hamilton or Dodge to draw from. My personal belief is that, when we enter into a flow state ,our consciousness extends into higher dimensions of possibility and is able to draw from the storehouse of wisdom that exists there. But let's not get too far ahead of ourselves, we will explore accessing higher dimensional wisdom in the next chapter.

I want to take a moment now to draw some interesting parallels found in Chinese philosophy. A number of years ago I read a book by Edward Slingerland called *Trying Not to Try*. I learned that there are interesting parallels between the flow states that we have been exploring here and the tradition of Chinese philosophy.

That book is essentially about the Chinese conception of Wu Wei, which as I see it is what we are exploring as flow in this book. Wu Wei can be translated as non-doing or perhaps we might define it as spontaneous effortless action. Slingerland's book opens with a traditional Chinese story about Butcher Ding. The awakened Butcher Ding was able to gracefully and effortlessly butcher an animal not because of his level of skill, but because he used more than his eyes or mind to do it. In his work, he connected with the task at hand invisibly and in doing so disengaged from the limitations of his physical senses and mental concepts. He entered into a spontaneous flow of activity that gave his actions an easeful precision that amazed everyone who witnessed them. This spontaneous flow of activity is Wu Wei.

In the state of Wu Wei, which I am equating with a state of flow, one gains access to capacities and wisdom from a mysterious source beyond. In Chinese philosophy differ thinkers have offered different explanations for where this state stems from. In the more conservative view of Confucius, what flows through us in our flow states is the composite wisdom that comes from the accumulated experience of our culture. In the view of Lao Tzu, the ultimate flow is universal and represents the way of the natural order of life. In order to become a true expression of the way, we must liberate ourselves from social conventions. When we liberate ourselves from all shaping influences and surrender to 'the way', we become an expression of universal currents of being – something like Emerson's Oversoul. We shall see in the next chapter that Lao Tzu's view has a great deal in common with the philosophical conceptions that were being explored and embodied by avant-garde artists in the 20th Century.

In all this talk of flow, I am reminded of a dance performance I once saw. In this particular performance, most of the dancers were very accomplished amateurs, but the last person to perform that night was the dance instructor of all the others. By the end of the night, when the instructor was about to start, I had already seen dozens of truly wonderful performances. Some I preferred to others for various reasons, but they were all truly magnificent in their own ways.

However, once the dance instructor began to dance, I was shocked. She was doing largely the same thing as everyone else, and in many ways, her dance was just one among others that night, except that it wasn't. There was something else happening in her dance and I could feel it. It was clearly and unmistakably obvious and yet I had no idea what it was. There was nothing that I was seeing in her performance that could account for what I was experiencing. The dance was so beautiful that I sat utterly transfixed through the entire performance. It wasn't what she was doing that was so mesmerizing, it was where she was doing it from that captivated me. What I saw was a dancer who was completely free, utterly let go and abandoned to her craft. The dance was happening, but there was nobody doing it. The dancer was connected to a source of inspiration that was dancing through her

15

and, like Butcher Ding, the liberated grace that she expressed was amazing. In the Chinese tradition, the amazement we feel when we witness someone operating in Wu Wei is known as De. De is a certain kind of magnetic charisma that a person in a state of Wu Wei always has. De is why we become transfixed by amazing performances.

Where does that special magnificence come from? In Steven Kottler's *The Rise of Superman*, he points us toward shifts that occur in brain functioning during flow states.

Normally when we are awake and active, there is a great deal of activity in the frontal cortex region of our brain. This is the part of the brain just behind your forehead where higher cognitive functions are controlled. This is where we think, analyze, and make decisions. It is the home of understanding. In a flow state, the frontal cortex gets very quiet, and the sense of self and all of our inner voices disappear along with it. As this occurs, our brainwaves shift from the high-speed beta wavelengths of waking consciousness down toward the alpha wavelengths of daydreaming, ultimately approaching the border of the theta wavelengths that we usually only experience just before we fall asleep. During a flow state, our consciousness rests at the border between alpha waves and theta waves, and that happens to be the place where our "aha" moments of insight are born. These flashes of insight are associated with bursts of brain activity that jump momentarily into the super high-speed gamma wavelength. These gamma bursts occur simultaneously with the bursts of spontaneous insight that come to us in flow. So, perhaps the miraculous insights of flow - Hamilton's hand drag or Dodge's escape fire - are the result of increased brain speed?

Although this explanation seems to satisfy our scientific curiosity about where the spontaneous wisdom of flow comes from, it doesn't really explain anything. We are still left with the question of where the insight of a gamma spike comes from. One plausible explanation might be that these super high-speed gamma bursts allow us to process information at much higher speeds than we normally can. This implies that the spontaneous wisdom of flow is produced through an increased ability to take in and process information. That is certainly a logical deduction, but I have to say that it doesn't feel completely satisfying to me because my own experience of spontaneous wisdom doesn't feel like just a matter of processing information faster. When I experience the explosive arising of insight, it feels like I am receiving information from a new source that wasn't previously available. That is why, as you will see in the next chapter, to me the metaphor of gaining access to higher dimensions of reality is more satisfying.

The brain science, however, is interesting to me for another reason. I am a teacher of meditation and deep states of meditation are also known to put our brains into the slow theta wavelengths where gamma bursts occur. When we meditate, we are consciously entering a theta wave state of brain functioning, similar to what we experience in sleep. This brainwave state is the place where gamma bursts originate. You might say that when we meditate, we are incubating inspired intuition.

If you are a meditator, you have almost certainly noticed that you occasionally have great ideas and powerful insights that appear out of nowhere. I often do, and sometimes they seem so amazing that I find it difficult to resist the temptation to stop and write them down. At the same time, I also don't want to engage my thinking mind and interrupt the inner flow state of meditation. I know that more insights will come, and I trust that any that are truly crucial will be remembered later.

What I find interesting about meditation is that I experience my practice as a flow state, but unlike the other flow states we have been discussing, this one doesn't involve any activity. The instructions for meditation that I teach and follow ask us only to *not do anything*. We simply allow whatever happens to happen without trying to interfere in any way. There is no activity to get lost in, so when you experience flow in meditation you are simply lost in the process of being alive. We will return to these more spiritual implications of flow in the last chapter of the book, but right now I have one last thing for us to consider about flow states.

One of the fascinating things about flow is that it appears to be contagious. What I mean by that is that not only can individuals experience flow, but it seems that groups can enter flow states together. A group of people in flow create and work together with a profound degree of precision and harmony. Think of a sports team working in perfect unison, or a musical band playing magnificently. In these states of group flow, a collective of individuals have a peak experience together. A group flow is more than individuals who are each in flow together, it is actually a flow state that moves the whole group of individuals into higher states of genius and intuition together as one. The rock musician Brian Eno used the term "scenius" to describe the kind of genius that emerges not from a single individual but from an entire scene. I believe that the American transcendentalists experienced scenius, as well as the artistic avant-garde in Paris in the 1920s. In these creative scenes, many of the individuals involved were carried by the collective energy of the group flow to higher realizations of brilliance.

Whether it happens in an individual or a group, a flow state is a state of emergence. In other words, what is so exciting about flow states is that wonderful and novel things emerge out of them. Ideas, insights, and capabilities are all generated freely in that state of being. Entering into a state of flow makes things possible for individuals and groups that would not be possible otherwise. This is why Steven Kotler sees flow states as a potential indicator of the future capacities of humanity. The capacities that we witness in people who are in flow are showing us the future, or at least the potential future, of our species.

As I see it, the key to entering flow states is being able to move our attention outside of our consciously deliberate and actively thinking mind. We can illustrate this with a simple example. There was an English boxer a few decades ago who made a big name for himself for a very short time. His fighting style was unorthodox, jerky, and unpredictable. He rose to a championship match quickly and won. For a time, he seemed to be unstoppable. He was knocking opponents out easily because no one could figure out his style or predict what he was going to do next. He would come into the ring, jerk and flutter and twist and turn, and suddenly a fist would fly out of the mayhem landing squarely on the opponent's jaw. Although I wasn't a big boxing fan, I found this fascinating, but it wasn't nearly as fascinating as what happened next.

I suppose it was inevitable, but of course he eventually got into the ring with someone who had watched enough video footage of him to figure out the style and come up with a plan to counter it. After a few minutes in the ring, the unorthodox champion got hit hard for the first time and something happened. Suddenly, all of the confidence drained from his eyes. He was scared. He no longer had the advantage of surprise. He was defeated handily that night.

As far as I know, he was never the same. The last time I saw him fighting, he was matched against a low-level opponent and yet, he still lost. In the world of sports, this is sometimes known as a slump. It happens to many players. They lose their confidence. They start overthinking everything and they spiral downward. Part of what allows any athlete to perform at their best is maintaining an unselfconscious state of flow. Only when we are able to operate without the hesitation imposed by the need for deliberation, does our performance flow smoothly, allowing our talents and training to naturally emerge as a spontaneous response to the demands of the moment.

What we have been exploring in this chapter is how flow states allow individuals and groups of individuals to optimally respond to circumstances and gain access to profound powers of creative genius. We have raised the obvious question of what exactly is the creative source that these amazing states of consciousness connect us with. We've talked about the corresponding brain states that emerge with flow, and I've alluded to my belief that we might be tapping into higher dimensions of reality. In the next chapter, we will explore the question of the creative source more carefully and relate that to how it is that cultures transform and evolve.

...success, like happiness, cannot be pursued; it must ensue...as the unintended side-effect of one's personal dedication to a course greater than oneself

~ MIHALY CSIKSZENTMIHALYI

02

The Illusion of Self and the Stream of Consciousness

"Those who flow as life flows know they need no other force."

~ LAO TZU

IN THE FIRST CHAPTER, we spoke about flow in terms of how it leads to greater human happiness and peak performance. In this chapter, we will add a third quality of flow – the potential for it to lead to profound transformation.

You see, the insights and actions that arise out of flow are often innovative and transformational. Laird Hamilton transformed the sport of big wave surfing, and Wag Dodge's life-saving intuition became a major innovation in firefighting. In a flow state, we tap into a source of wisdom that lies beyond our conditioned ways of thinking and previous knowledge. This allows us to bring novelty into the world that can transform ourselves and the society we live in.

So now we turn our attention to how flow states have been explored as a force of social and cultural change. By their very nature, cultures are governed by rules and norms. Some of these are conscious and others are unconscious. I don't want to make this sound like a bad thing, quite the opposite in fact. In many ways, the rules and norms of a culture support harmonious and fruitful human interaction. For example, we have strict rules about which side of the road we must drive on, and it's very useful that, for the most part, people adhere to them. There is very little value to be gained in deciding to spontaneously drive on the wrong side of the road.

It is important to realize that the novelty that emerges in flow is shaped to some degree by our past experience and previous knowledge. Laird Hamilton had a great deal of experience and knowledge of surfing that undoubtedly, and perhaps unconsciously, informed his spontaneous insight to drag his hand in the water. Similarly, Wag Dodge was not just anyone running from a fire, he was a highly trained and experienced firefighter.

The art of improvisation gives us a wonderful metaphor for understanding flow and how our skills and talents play a part in what emerges through flow. The best improvisation in jazz and theater is done by individuals who are highly trained and talented. Of course, and somewhat paradoxically, the magic that creates the genius of improvisational flow is the ability to allow things to arise spontaneously in the moment without prior thought or planning. In other words, the best improvisation is done by individuals that are highly trained, but the key to great improvisation is performing beyond our training.

I experienced this potential in a fascinating way

when I was experimenting with theatrical improvisation. What I felt is that I was carried away by a character I was playing, and I didn't know where the lines I was speaking were coming from. It happened during an improvisation workshop where a small group of us were acting out a scene that was supposed to happen in an architect's office. The scene starts with us discussing the plans for a new project when all of a sudden one of the actors shouted, "Where did the plans go?" They were obviously alarmed and without thinking I responded, "I just saw Franny walk out the door with them a minute ago." I was completely amazed by what I'd said because it hadn't felt like something that I'd made up. It felt like the truth. I honestly felt like I had said it because I actually knew that Franny had walked off with the plans. In truth, there was no one named Franny among us, but still it felt like there was. I even had a distinct memory of seeing her walk out of the door with the plans under her arm.

What was going on there? How did those words and those feelings and memories appear in me? In the end, the best way I can describe it is to say that they were produced by the scene itself. The scene seemed to pull the words out of my mouth and then it supplied me with the exact feelings and memories I needed to convincingly support them. We will return to this idea that a scene can pull things out of people soon, so keep this image in mind for later, but for now I hope you see that this brings a whole new level of meaning to Brian Eno's idea of scenius.

After that experience, I started to wonder what the difference was between me being that character in an imagined scene and me being Jeff in the role I play in my real life. In many ways, it doesn't seem like there is much of a difference. Could it be that the character of Jeff is just as much an improvisation, but one that I am so used to, or so completely in flow with, that it feels like the real me? I wondered how long I would need to play a different character before that felt like the real me.

I share all this to make a point. Flow is a source of happiness that can inspire achievement and creative genius, and because it injects novelty into the normal flow of life, it can also be transformative. Now we will examine how a number of artists and intellectuals in the middle of the 20th century explored how acts of spontaneous creation might transform culture.

Daniel Belgrad's fascinating book, *The Culture of Spontaneity*, gives us a historical portrait of the artistic scene that arose in New York city during the years post World War II. That time period saw the emergence of ideologies and philosophies that redefined art and the artist's role in instigating culture change.

In Belgrad's book, I saw a group of people working to articulate a new human possibility. These visionaries were working in a matrix of mutual influence, inspiring and informing each other as part of a pioneering community of explorers. In other words, they were part of an artistic scene. They were not articulating something that had already existed but was hidden from view; they were creating something that had not existed before by giving it life through the expressive media of their different arts.

I believe that the power of spontaneous creativity reveals something profound about our co-creative relationship with the world we live in and the truly multi-dimensional nature of reality itself. To get a sense of what I mean by this, we must be willing to consider the possibility that we live in a very thin slice of a reality that is vastly larger and more multi-dimensional than what we can even begin to perceive.

It is my belief that there are many dimensions of reality that affect us even though we can't perceive them. Our perceptions of reality are restricted to a very limited number of its dimensions, in a way similar to how our eyes can only see the tiniest band of the vast electromagnetic spectrum. We see so little of reality and yet we often think we understand the whole of it. Generally speaking, human beings have a tendency to assume that we see a much greater portion of what is real than we likely are.

Imagine a two-dimensional reality. That would mean an entire universe that was perfectly flat like a tabletop. This kind of universe was dubbed Flatland by Edwin A. Abbott in his classic book, *Flatland: A Romance of Many Dimensions*, first published in 1884.

If you lived in this flat reality, everything would appear as a line because the space above or below the line exists in dimensions beyond the universe of Flatland.

If a sphere, which is a three-dimensional object, were to pass through Flatland, it would float up through the flat surface of the tabletop, but a flatlander would only be able to see the line of the sphere's edge as it passed by. In Flatland, you would have no idea of the parts of the sphere that existed above or below the line because they literally exist outside of your universe. The infinite space above and below the flat surface of Flatland is nonexistent to Flatlanders.

In our world, we exist in three dimensions of space and so the addition of a fourth dimension of space is impossible for us to imagine; it is beyond comprehension. Go ahead, try to imagine what a fourth dimension of space would look like. If a fourth dimension of space were to exist, it would spread infinitely in a new and unimaginable dimension of existence. If there were five, six, seven, or more dimensions beyond the three that we know, how foolish does it start to feel to assume we know anything at all about the nature of reality?

Some spiritual experiences that I've had have led me to the firm personal conviction that we exist in a three-dimensional cross section of a much larger multi-dimensional reality, and that we, *ourselves*, exist in more than three dimensions (even though we normally only experience three dimensions of ourselves).

We are multi-dimensional beings and I believe that acts of spontaneous creation are sometimes expressions of higher dimensional aspects of who we are. The reason that I wrote this book is because I believe that flow states can give us access to our higher-dimensional creative potentials.

What I found in Belgrad's book about the American post-war artistic culture was a group of creative individuals, philosophers, psychologists, artists, dancers, potters, and writers, who were inspired by a vision very similar to this. They were inspiring each other, driven by a vision of reality that was being derived from: the new physics of relativity, Carl Jung's idea of the collective unconscious, the philosophy of existentialism, and the process philosophy articulated by Alfred North Whitehead. This vision was not only inspired by ideas; it was coming directly from the actual experience that these artists were having in creating their art.

When we speak about culture change, I think it can be useful to think in terms of the evolution of consciousness. If we want to think about how consciousness evolves and grows, it can be helpful to think in terms of a larger being of which we are a part. Imagine that there is a larger higher-dimensional being that is continually bringing more and more of itself into manifestation in our three-dimensional universe. I like to refer to that larger being as a meta-being, a term I borrowed from the feminist theologian Mary Daly.

In my own spiritual journey, some of the most important breakthrough experiences that I had were experiences of what I would call collective awakening. In these experiences, I was part of small groups of people who all had the unmistakable experience of having a higher consciousness speaking through us. With a great deal of work and preparation, we found that it was possible to allow something bigger than us to emerge in dialog. We felt as if we had collectively become the passageway for a higher consciousness. We stepped aside and let something larger than us take over. This may seem difficult to believe, but those experiences are just as alive and compelling for me today as they were nearly twenty years ago when I originally had them.

The experiences of collective awakening that I've had left me strongly convinced that there was a larger being, a meta-being or a higher-dimensional being, emerging into and through our three-dimensional universe. That higher being wants to be fully brought into manifestation, and when we articulate our deep spiritual realizations, we become a vehicle for that higher being, playing a role in bringing its energy, intelligence, and love into the world of time and space.

This is my spiritual orientation. It is the best way I know of to articulate what my own spiritual experiences over the past thirty years have revealed to me about the nature of reality. I try to not be too literal about it, and I understand that this may not be the way you've come to see things. This is simply the way I've come to see things and I would never want you to simply adopt my way of seeing. All I ask is that you take an honest look at what I am sharing in this book to see if it resonates with you. See if it reveals a trail of experiences from your own life that point to the very same possibility. It is very likely that you will resonate with this vision because, after all, you did choose to read this book.

When I read Daniel Belgrad's *The Culture of Spontaneity*, I was introduced to an alternative spiritual tradition that was being lived and developed by creative individuals in the wake of the Second World War in and around New York City. Many of the ideas that I found these luminaries were inspired by matched the conclusions that I had come to. I saw that, without knowing it, I was part of a line of inspired individuals who were using the power of spontaneous action to bring new possibilities into the world.

If you trace a line backward in time, you will find a clear connection between this alternative spiritual tradition and the teachings of Ralph Waldo Emerson in Concord, Massachusets. First of all, the artists and writers that Belgrad discusses were influenced by the avant-garde of Paris in preceding decades. Gertrude Stein was a central figure in that scene and a personal mentor to many of the individuals in it. She was also a protégé of William James who was deeply influenced by his godfather Ralph Waldo Emerson. In addition, the philosopher Alfred North Whitehead, who was part of the inspiration of the New York group, followed James as the chair of philosophy at Harvard and would refer to William James as his master. In future books, I intend to outline the growth of this alternative spiritual lineage in detail, but for now we will stay focused on the New York avant-garde.

When I read Belgrad's book, I found it fascinating that I had been pursuing alternative spiritual ideas for decades, and although I'd heard of many of the people mentioned in the book, no one had ever put the story together in a way that allowed me to see it as a true lineage of spiritual and cultural creation. The ideas that these creative luminaries were exploring were radical and revolutionary. I began to suspect that, because they pose a threat to the foundations of the dominant paradigm, they have become largely hidden from view. Of course, they are not hidden in the sense of being out of site, many of the people are famous, but they have become effectively hidden in plain site because they were labeled as fringe outliers that were interesting but not ultimately consequential to mainstream society.

Those of us who are pursuing alternative spiritual ideas are left without a history to draw strength from. The so-called New Age movement that so many people have written about remains perpetually new, regardless of how many people have explored similar ideas for decades and even centuries. In order to maintain its dominance, the current paradigm will always suppress any alternative points of view. I am not meaning to say that anyone is consciously doing this, it is more of an unconscious movement of self-preservation that happens instinctually at a cultural level. We are led to falsely believe that the ideas that inspire us are new, having only recently emerged. By denying this alternative culture a sense of its history, the movement is robbed of its power, doomed to experience itself as the perpetual newcomer on the scene, lacking experience and influence. It serves the preservation of the dominant paradigm if those who are actively seeking an alternative are isolated from and ignorant of each other. Recognizing ourselves to be part of an identifiable lineage is deeply empowering. And that is exactly the experience I had reading Belgrad's book.

The cultural movement in post-war New York was part of the larger current of cultural change that began with the Romantic revolution in the 18th century. The German poet Johann Wolfgang von Goethe is often recognized as the progenitor of that movement – although in the end he distanced himself from it. As I have already stated, Romanticism was a response to some of the negative effects of the Enlightenment, such as the destructive effects of industrialization and the mob that took over the French Revolution.

As a result of this new movement, a new way of thinking began to emerge in Europe and America. The individuals engaged in this new thinking no longer saw the universe as a mechanical clock that ticked unthinkingly and unfeelingly along according to the dictates of natural law. Instead, these new thinkers, empowered by the emerging science of biology, saw the entire universe as a living being that was inherently creative. The ideas that emerged at this time have been alive ever since, although often hidden in plain sight, and Belgrad tells us the story of how they reemerged in the middle of the 20th century.

In the years after World War II, an artistic movement was born in New York City and later moved to the Hamptons of Long Island where rent, at least at the time, was less expensive. The catastrophic destruction of the war had ignited a passion for deep change in many people and that passion emerged as a powerful artistic and intellectual movement. As has often been the case in human history, catastrophic circumstances led people to conclude that the structures that maintain our world are so deficient that they must be replaced at the deepest level with a new vision of reality. The art of this movement includes: the poetry of William Carlos Willliams, and later Jack Kerouac, Allen Ginsberg, Joyce Johnson, and Diane di Prima of the Beat Generation. Working at the same time was a group of artists that became known as the Abstract Expressionists who were working with the same ideas on canvas. These artists included Willem De Kooning, Jackson Pollock, Helen Frankenthaler, and my own good friend Nicole Bigar. This revolution in creative expression was not just limited to poets and artists. The philosopher and psychologist, Paul Goodman, was a central figure in the scene as well. And Black Mountain College with its eclectic mix of potters, poets, teachers, and pioneering thinkers also became an important incubator for these new ideas.

This emerging thinking was deeply influenced by the psychologist Carl Jung and, specifically, by his vision of the collective unconscious. The alternative thinkers in New York embraced the idea of the collective unconscious as a vast storehouse of hidden human wisdom and potential. The myths and archetypes that exist in that shared unconscious realm shape us, sometimes in limiting ways, but perhaps, they speculated, in liberating ways. What if we could access the hidden wisdom of the collective unconscious to unearth possibilities that lie beyond our individual limitations? What if we could express ourselves freely without the influence of the guardrails of social and cultural assumptions? This possibility for radically free expression is what the culture of spontaneity was exploring. They wanted to know how to express freely from the deepest wells of human wisdom and love.

The creative methodology that these luminaries embraced was spontaneous expression. They strove in their art to express spontaneously from a mysterious inner source that was beyond comprehension. They wanted to create from a place so deep in the psyche that it had yet to be conditioned by cultural assumptions. They wanted to unleash radical creative freedom.

Carl Jung also introduced the idea of "participation mystique" into the shared ideology of the movement. This is a fascinating notion that recognizes that the human beings of earlier cultures did not experience themselves as distinctly separate and isolated from each other and the world in the same way that modern humans do. Modern society cultivates a deeply individuated sense of self. Jung and others realized that there have been, and are, cultures on Earth in which this is not the case. In these cultures, individuals are less differentiated, less individuated, and less separate. They are more enmeshed with nature, with the world, and with each other. In these more embedded cultures, consciousness has a different flavor. It connects and interpenetrates with all of reality. Participation mystique, or "mystical participation", originally conceived by the French scholar Lucien Lévy-Bruhl, was a term used to describe this highly participatory consciousness.

In the consciousness of participation mystique, people experience themselves as embedded in the environment. They are partially individuated and distinguishable, but not fully separate from the world they live in. This consciousness has a dream-like quality in which you exist in concert with other beings as part of the community of the natural world. You are one aspect of the circumstances that surround you.

I see something in the consciousness of participation mystique that once again mirrors my own
spiritual experiences. What I have seen in powerful
experiences of revelation is that the experience of consciousness, when it is rooted in separation and duality,
is crisp and clear with sharp edges of division and distinction. But the consciousness of unity, which I am
associating with participation mystique, feels dreamier
because the boundaries that divide things are not as
clear. Our awareness is more blended. There's more
bleed-through between me and you, between me and
the world.

In participation mystique, we don't experience
ourselves as a completely separate source of power that
can impose itself upon nature. Instead, we are just one
of the factors of influence in nature; we have partial,
but not full control over what occurs. We don't see
ourselves residing in the seat of causality. We have
some influence over what happens, but we are also
affected by many forces greater than us. This way of
operating in the world is more like surfing on a wave
rather than driving down the highway. In a car, you
have the power of a self-contained vehicle to propel
yourself forward. You're in control of the movement.
When you're surfing, your movement is being powered by a wave that you do not control as it moves
beneath your board. When you drive, you're moved
by your own power, your own engine, and your fuel
source. When you surf, you're carried along by forces

beyond your control that you have to understand and navigate.

The term participation mystique seems to extend the metaphor of surfing to all of life. The individuals that were part of this revolution in consciousness recognized the possibility of entering into conscious participation with the deeper forces of creation. The possibility of creating from a spontaneous state of flow became the driving intention of their art. They aspired to remove the dividing lines that separate the artist from their art and establish a direct line of communication between themselves and the inspired source of their creations. They wanted to let go, open up, and let the art flow through them from a mysterious source.

According to Belgrad's book, another powerful influence on the New York movement came from the Harvard philosopher Alfred North Whitehead. Whitehead was an English mathematician and philosopher who famously worked with Bertrand Russell, but after he retired from his academic position in England, he was offered the chair of philosophy position at Harvard University and accepted it. Whitehead continued to work at Harvard for another ten years, and during that time, he wrote many books that outlined his vision of process philosophy. It was his vision of life as a series of ongoing processes that was so influential to the artists in New York in the postwar era.

Whitehead was a mathematician inspired by

Einstein's theory of relativity and the new physics that was emerging at the start of the 20th century. And he was busy constructing a new vision of cosmology to match the advances in our scientific understanding of the universe. Albert Einstein had introduced a conception of space and time vastly different from the classical ideas of Newtonian physics. Newtonian space is an infinite expanse that spreads endlessly in three directions, up and down, left and right, forward and backward. Our consciousness and our way of perceiving reality is shaped by this view of three-dimensional empty space extending in all directions and that exists independent of anything that happens to reside in it.

Einstein was saying something different. Space and time are not uniformly spread in all directions. The don't exist always and everywhere the same. There are circumstances under which time speeds up or slows down, or where space contracts or expands. The theory of general relativity explains that gravity is not a force that acts between objects through a constant field of space and time. Instead, the phenomena that we know of as gravity is actually caused because space and time, now called spacetime, bend and contort around solid objects like planets and stars. The reason things move faster as they get closer to a planet is not because some force is pulling hard on them. It's because space is scrunching up, and time is shortening. This is a dramatically different way of understanding reality than Newton ever dreamed of.

Whitehead was very enticed by this, and he wanted to create a philosophy that described reality more like an energetic field than a physical place. What we experience as 'things' are actually energetic phenomena that arise in a field of being, not physical objects. That means that this table in front of me is a point of convergence for energies that exist in the field of being. Those energies don't exist just here at this point of convergence, they exist throughout reality. The energies that make up anything exist everywhere, but at a particular point they congeal and converge, they scrunch up, into what we experience as a solid object. Human beings are not things that exist separate from other things. We are a convergence point of energies and forces that exist throughout space and time but gather densely in us.

This is very difficult to imagine because it contradicts the Newtonian assumptions that our perception has been conditioned by. The artists that Belgrad discusses were interested in these ideas, which at least some of them had found in Whitehead's book *Adventures of Ideas*, where he discusses how ideas shape human history. In Whitehead's philosophy, we find a new way to speak about reality. We stop speaking in terms of objects in space, and instead we speak about occasions, events, or happenings. We are not things, we are happenings, occurrences that arises freshly in each moment. We are events that continuously unfold. Everything is a perpetually unfolding process, hence the name process philosophy.

The artists and visionaries that were inspired by this vision began seeing a possibility for a new reality. If reality was not made of solid things, but occurrences of convergence, then perhaps more change was possible than we ever imagined. Could we change the way energies converged so that something different and new would emerge? I believe this was exciting to them because they were seeing spontaneous creation in their art as a way of directly participating in the creation of a new reality.

In their art and poetry, they wanted to deemphasize the product, and emphasize the process. They wanted to enter the process of creative emergence and allow themselves to be overtaken by it. They did not want to merely recreate the visions they had in their minds on canvas or in words. They wanted to let go of everything they thought and allow the art or poem to be created in a flurry of spontaneous engagement.

My friend Nicole Bigar was part of the circle of artists who moved from Manhattan to Long Island. She described to me how many of them would remain in silence before they started painting, waiting to be moved. When the creative energy started to flow, they would surrender to it and allow it to move them through the artistic process. The painting would emerge through them, and they would strive not to interfere with the process as it unfolded. Sometimes they were successful and witnessed the creation of a piece of art that had come from some place beyond them.

The poet Charles Olson articulated this idea when he wrote about what he called "composition by field." As I see it, Olson wanted to spontaneously write poetry so that the words would come out faster than thought. In that way, he imagined that the words were coming directly from the energetic field of being itself. By creating from beyond his conscious mind and thought processes, he hoped to become a vehicle for a spontaneous expression of higher possibilities. He didn't know what he was writing; he was just letting the writing happen through him. The words themselves were sourced from a deeper place.

The famous abstract painter Jackson Pollock wanted to eliminate any separation between himself and his art. He wanted to paint from inside the painting, so he used huge pieces of canvas spread on the floor. In this way, he could engage with the canvas from all sides even walking straight over it. He was painting from as close to inside the painting as he could get. He was embedded and enmeshed with the process of painting as it unfolded.

To these artists and poets, a work of art was not just a thing created by the skill and effort of the artist. Art emerged out of a deep process of communion between the artist and the process of creation. The artist initiated the process, but they didn't control it. For them, part of what makes something art is that it has a life of its own. The artwork affects the artist as much as the artist affects the work. Your painting, or your poem, or your pottery, is creating you as you are creating it. The art speaks to you, giving you insights and intuitions that are then folded back into the art. It's a process of mutual collaboration between the art and the artist.

It was not only in the domain of artistic expressions that this co-creative process was recognized. Paul Goodman, who was one of the founders of Gestalt therapy, wanted to break down the wall separating the therapist and the client, and do away with the image of a patient lying on a couch while a detached therapist listens and gives advice. Instead, he, along with Fritz Perls and others, developed a view of therapy as an encounter between a therapist and a client. In that encounter, insights emerge spontaneously in the moment. The therapist is not simply applying what they already know about psychological theory. They are meeting the client free from preconceptions and allowing clarity to reveal itself through the immediacy of interaction.

What we are seeing in this cultural movement is experimentation with a new way of being human. Rather than action through conscious deliberation according to the ideas held in the mind, these cultural pioneers were exploring the possibility of acting spontaneously and releasing conscious control so that an intelligence beyond their own mind could reveal itself.

Through spontaneous expression, they hoped to tap into sources of creativity that were ungoverned and unlimited by the conscious mind.

In reading about the explorations of this artistic circle, I am reminded of the term *between-ness* that I first heard from an American spiritual teacher named Richard Rose. Between-ness is a consciousness that lies in the space between total intention and complete detachment from outcome. When the focus and intensity of intention is applied at the very same time that there is no attachment to a specific outcome, the magical mental state of between-ness is entered. In my experience, that space is a gateway to deeper creativity. Between-ness is a place that exists between all pairs of opposites. In that place, I am neither here nor there, neither asleep nor awake. Or perhaps I could say that I am both here and there, asleep and awake. My experiences of between-ness sound very similar to Participation Mystique.

In the open frame of mind of between-ness, the separation and divisions that are usually so clear become indistinct. I can't be as certain about where this thing ends, and another begins. The line that separates the past from the future blurs so that I become uncertain if there is any difference at all between them. It's a space which feels permeable and dreamy. It's a place where things that seem magical become possible and where I am able to perceive and articulate realities that shouldn't exist. This space is what I believe has inspired great art and genius throughout the ages. It is where we gain access to the impossible, so that we can bring it into existence. It is the place where transformation takes place.

Don't ask what the world needs. Ask what makes you come alive. Because what the world needs most is more people who have come alive.

- HOWARD THURMAN

03

Spiritual Liberation and the Joy of Self-Forgetting

*"There is an ecstasy that marks the summit
of life, and beyond which life cannot rise.
And such is the paradox of living,
this ecstasy comes when one is most alive,
and it comes as a complete forgetfulness
that one is alive."*

- JACK LONDON

IN THIS FINAL CHAPTER, I want to share my thoughts about what I see as the ultimate potential of flow, namely the part that it plays in unlocking our true potential for radical spiritual awakening and transformation. Ultimately, for me, this is what makes flow states so significant. They are part of the mechanism that allows us to break out of our habitual ways of perceiving so we can open up to an entirely novel possibility for human life.

Let's start this inquiry with a simple assertion, we are self-aware. We don't just experience the world; we experience ourselves experiencing it.

In this chapter, we will explore the process of spiritual growth and see how it includes both an expansion of self-awareness and a process of self-forgetting. Through our spiritual work, we gain a deeper awareness of the larger, previously hidden dimensions of ourselves, and at the same time we gradually release our hypnotic fascination with the more limited aspects of self.

Over the past few hundred years, particularly in Western culture, we've been very busy developing a strong and stable sense of self. We've built up a powerful cultural capacity to hold an abstract image of ourselves and use it as an ever-present reference point. What this means is that we've learned how to create a strong idea of who we are. Our self-image includes a story about our history, knowledge of our personal strengths and weaknesses, preferences, attitudes, etc. All of these elements are amalgamated into a sense of the person that I am. This is the highly individuated modern sense of self that we spoke about in the last chapter.

We are taught to identify with our self-image, to assume that the ideas we hold about ourselves create a more or less accurate picture of who we are. They don't. They only describe a few aspects of who we are, and often even those are wrong. It is important to recognize that our self-image is not who we are, it is just a set of ideas; a mental model we use to represent ourselves to our ourselves in our own minds. A strong and healthy self-image is very useful and even crucial in many ways, but we are more than that, we are not just a set of ideas, and the ideas we hold about ourselves can only describe a very small part of who we are.

In our culture, we've been taught to assume that we are the person portrayed by our self-image. That means that we are the person that was born on our birthday, has lived our history, and who has a specific set of characteristics and attitudes. When we look out at the world, we assume that it is the person defined by our self-image that is doing the looking. When we look at ourselves, we assume that there are two of us, the one who is looking and the one who we see. This is what it commonly means to be self-aware. We think that self-aware means being aware of yourself, but usually it means being aware of ideas about yourself; it means being aware of your self-image. What we commonly imagine to be self-awareness, is really self-concept-awareness.

Spiritual awakening and growth, as I am using the terms here, means waking up to the fullness of your being beyond the limits of self-concept. It means opening up to the true vastness of your being. Spiritual work is a retraining of attention. We gradually learn to pay less attention to our self-concept, and as we do, we begin to get a sense that we are much more than that. In common vernacular, people speak in terms of letting go of the small self and embracing the big Self. In this chapter, I am asserting that flow states play a crucial role in this shift of identity from the small self to the big Self.

A self-concept or self-identity has to be something that we can distinguish from the rest of the world – it has to be identifiable; it has to be separate. We have become almost entirely identified with our individuated and separate sense of self. We assume that the image of ourselves that we created in our minds is who we are. We assume that we know who we are. Of course, we don't know everything about ourselves. There is always more self-knowledge to be gained, but fundamentally we know who all that self-knowledge is about. We know ourselves. We are self-aware.

The journey of awakening that I have devoted my life to is a journey from self-awareness to Self-awareness. It's a journey from only identifying with the parts of yourself that you can see, to the realization that who you really are is vaster than can be known and inseparable from life itself. One of the things that stands in the way of this profound realization is our current understanding of what it means to be conscious. We are so infatuated by our human self-awareness that we tend to equate it with consciousness itself. That means that if there are aspects of ourselves that we cannot see, we naturally assume that they don't really exist.

Spiritual realizations always come in the form of ineffable flashes of insight. They are not deduced logically. They appear spontaneously as a knowing that cannot be traced to a cause. We just know something, and we don't know how we know it. We have an inexplicable experience of certainty about something that we can't perceive in any ordinary sense. This is why spiritual revelations are said to be mysterious. These flashes of certainty feel totally real and true, and yet you can't put your finger on them, or explain them to anyone else. Most of us, at least occasionally, have these intuitions, and most of us find it difficult to trust them. More often than not, we slowly lose faith in them until we end up dismissing them as misunderstandings or mistakes.

If we don't know how we know something, if we can't be aware of being aware of it, if we can't see ourselves seeing it, then we tend to doubt that it exists. Self-conscious awareness is the form of consciousness we've learned to trust. We need the evidence of being aware of ourselves being aware, and knowing how we know, before we can trust what we see and what we understand.

As I have come to see it, this is the biggest spiritual challenge that we must overcome on the path to spiritual liberation. Why? Because the miraculous revelations of spirit that reveal a deeper truth come to us from beyond our current sense of self. What they reveal are wider dimensions of reality, dimensions that exist beyond our self-image, dimensions that our current sense of self will never see. What is miraculous is that, even though our sense of self cannot see these immaculate visions, we can still be aware of them. The mysterious nature of them is not evidence that they do not exist, the mystery is showing us that our current perception of our self is not the limit of who we are.

As I have come to understand it, spiritual awakening is the sudden realization that you are more than who you thought you were. You are more than the person that was born on your birthday and will live on this planet for an as yet undisclosed length of time.

You are a vast multi-dimensional confluence of energies of which you can only see the slimmest part. Spiritual growth, on the other hand, involves the never-ending gradual process of learning to trust the parts of yourself that you cannot see. In this process of Self-trust, we learn to listen with inner ears, and see blindly into the darkness of the unknown. As we do, we hear the subtle insight and wisdom that stream from our deeper heart, we see the expansive visions of a reality that exist beyond what our physical eyes are able to see and our brains could ever know.

The key to spiritual growth is learning to trust. It involves gaining the increasing humility necessary to accept that there is more to reality than we've ever known and will ever know. Reality is a mystery beyond the comprehensive powers of the small self, but not beyond the intuitive knowing faculty of your True Self. You gain access to the sweeping mysteries of being by letting go of your strict adherence to the perceptual limitations of the small self and expanding into the greater totality of who you are.

This is why I say that spiritual growth can also be understood as a loss of self-awareness. In this sense, it is not only about discovering who we really are, but also about ceasing to be distracted by any limited part of ourselves. As you allow your attention to drift beyond your limited sense of self, you encounter strange new possibilities that you cannot understand. By letting go of the part of yourself that experiences-itself-experiencing, the *self-conscious self* we could say, we become more and more absorbed in direct contact with the process of life as it unfolds.

As we grow spiritually, we enter more and more deeply into a flow state with being alive.

But because we tend to define awareness in terms that the *self-aware self* can understand, we find it difficult to be satisfied with an awakening that we cannot see ourselves having. We don't just want to be free; we want to *know* that we are free. We want to watch the movie of our own spiritual liberation as we are having it. This is the biggest hindrance we face on the path to spiritual liberation.

The profound, arguably cruel, cosmic joke of the spiritual path is that you will eventually realize that as soon as you let go of the need to know that you're awake, you will discover that you already are and always have been awake. You already are having a direct, immediate, unmitigated experience of reality. You are already free of the small self's distorting influence that creates the sense of separation from life. You have always been in flow with being alive. In fact, all you are is the flow of life.

Once you see this, it will be obvious that you have always been aware of it and you have always known it. But you cannot be aware of yourself and that at the same time. You cannot pass into direct contact with life and hold on to your self-conscious self simultaneously. The passageway is too narrow. Your sense of self will not fit. This is the eye of the needle that is the gateway to heaven. Nothing can squeeze through with you. There is a classic spiritual metaphor that describes this: A monkey squeezes its hand through a small hole in a heavy box to grab a banana that has been placed there. With its hand clenching the banana he cannot get his hand back out and because he won't let go of the banana, he is trapped.

On the razor-sharp edge of direct contact with life, there is no room for a self-image. There just is what is, and you are nothing but that. The experience of the small self is created in the separation with the edge. On the edge, there is no experience of a small self. On the edge, you can only experience life. You cannot experience yourself experiencing it. Just like in flow states.

This insight, if you let it, will flip everything upside down and radically change everything without anything at all needing to be different. This is the ultimate paradigm shift.

When we seek spiritual liberation, we might think that we are seeking happiness, or wisdom, or super capacities, but what we really want is to be free from the human-centered limitations of our consciousness. We want to be free from our ideas about ourselves, so we can come into direct contact with life and embody the fullness of ourselves. This freedom is what ultimately drives the passion for extreme sports. Laird Hamilton is quoted explicitly in *The Rise of Superman* describing his otherworldly spiritual experiences in flow. This is the same freedom that the avant-garde of Paris and New York wanted to explore and harness for the world's benefit. Beneath all of our passion for flow states is our passion to be one with the process of life.

The part of us that is aware of ourselves in consciousness is our sense of self, our self-concept, our self-image. When we define consciousness exclusively in terms of the consciousness of our self-image, then consciousness becomes a property owned by the sense of self. Consciousness, we wrongly assume, belongs to the small self rather than to existence itself. The consciousness of the universe has become trapped inside our self-image. That package is too tight. It is suffocating. We feel that sense of suffocation and that is what drives us to the spiritual path in the first place.

Spiritual liberation is the liberation of consciousness from exclusive adherence to the perspective of our small sense of self.

The ultimate promise of spiritual liberation is that the profound creative potential that human beings have been developing for so long will finally be at the service of existence itself. Remember, spiritual liberation implies freeing the spirit. Spiritual liberation unleashes our spirit. Suddenly, we are inspired, powered, and driven by a universal source of wisdom and love rather than smaller self-concerns.

When the smaller self's concerns become less daunting and preoccupying to us, the concerns of existence start to move and circulate within us. The truly miraculous self-aware consciousness that we worked so hard to develop will not disappear, it will simply become available for a universal being. The most compelling reason to pursue spiritual liberation is to allow the true creative potential of the human spirit to become available to serve universal concerns.

In this chapter, I am encouraging you to think about spiritual liberation as a special kind of flow state because when we are in flow, we become one with the unfolding process of life. We may do things, but we are not aware of doing them. We don't feel like we are doing them. We feel like they are just happening.

There are many domains in which I have experienced the magic of flow. When I write, I often get into a flow state and find that I've written for an hour and can't remember what I wrote. I go back and read it and think, "Wow, who wrote this?"

I also paint, and sometimes my brush just flows over the canvas and amazing shapes and colors appear in front of my eyes. They were not something I planned to create and, once they appear, I don't know where they came from either.

And finally, I've trained and practiced in the spiritual art of Ancient Lomi Lomi, a shamanic form of massage. What I have discovered in that art, when I manage to truly let go, is that the massage is not guided by my mind. It is guided by a wisdom that arises directly out of the sensation of touch itself. I don't feel like I know what I'm doing. I'm not following a plan or applying techniques. I feel like I'm acting in service of a massage that wants to happen.

One of the primary characteristics of flow is that you forget yourself. You get so absorbed in what you're doing that you lose awareness of yourself doing it. You lose self-awareness, and when that happens? You feel free!

Spiritual liberation is a special kind of flow state because it occurs when we're not doing anything in particular. In normal flow states, we get absorbed in a particular activity. It could be skateboarding, knitting, dancing, tennis, etc. In most ordinary flow states, there is something that captivates our attention deeply enough to allow us to forget ourselves.

The experience of spiritual liberation is a state of flow that doesn't have a focusing activity. You are just in flow with living.

Meditation, at least the way I teach it, is a practice that is ripe for igniting the special flow state of spiritual liberation. If you sit in meditation and allow yourself to become absorbed in the experience of being, all of your attention will be consumed by the miracle of awareness and the process of life. You forget about yourself. You are just absorbed in being aware. Eventually you forget about yourself being absorbed in anything, and the only thing left is awareness.

If you spend enough time resting in the inherent wonder of being in this way, you start to forget how you used to watch yourself. You become so absorbed in being that it becomes your natural state. When I have been lucky enough to experience this on long retreats, I found myself walking around, in between sessions of meditation, not sure of who I was and not knowing who was doing anything.

In this open state of mind, I am profoundly available to be moved by the love and wisdom of existence itself. I've stopped directing life and I'm available to receive greater insight, intuition, and compassion. The separate sense of being me is no longer the one seeing through my eyes, feeling my emotions, or generating the wisdom that continually arises in my mind.

My experiences of this sacred flow state with life have left me certain that the spiritual liberation we seek is not our own. Without realizing it, we have always been seeking to liberate the higher possibilities that lay hidden inside us. There is a new way of being that is waiting to be born and our spiritual freedom begins the process of its birth.

Human life is a spiritual path that can lead to the gradual expansion of a Self-awareness that belongs to existence itself, not to us alone. How conscious we are of that process varies from person to person and moment to moment. Generally speaking, at the beginning, we travel the path of awakening without realizing it, and therefore the path is somewhat random and haphazard. We increase Self-awareness in fits and starts; we have a breakthrough here, fall back there, one life circumstance provides a growth opportunity, another pushes us into contraction and fear.

Eventually, we wake up to the process of spiritual growth and realize that we are on a spiritual path. Once we begin to consciously engage with the path of awakening, we feel compelled to understand the mechanisms of growth and engage in behaviors and practices that will optimally align us with those mechanisms.

Spiritual work is like surfing a huge ocean wave. You need to understand the forces that are moving you and align your board and balance in ways that allow you to be stable and steady as you are propelled forward by the power surging through the wave. In the same way, the spiritual aspirant becomes intimately familiar with the spiritual movements and forces that propel them forward into ever-greater Self-awareness.

An important question that must be asked in this process is who exactly is it that's becoming more Self-aware? Is it me, Jeff, the person who was born on my birthday and has lived my life since then? Or does the experience of Self-awareness belong to something bigger than me from the start? As I see it, our individual spiritual growth is a small part of a much larger process of spiritual growth.

There is a larger being, a meta-being, that is coming into greater Self-awareness and our spiritual growth is a part of that larger awakening process. Our spiritual yearnings are the stirrings of a higher order of being that is endeavoring to know itself more fully through us. As we embrace all of who we are, we allow this larger being to discover itself and ultimately, we realize that we are that. It is not us who is waking up; a miraculous possibility of an entirely new way of being is waking up through us.

We are more than just a single biological entity living with billions of other separate individuals on the surface of a planet. Our life is emerging from the living source of an entire universe that is perpetually in the middle of the process of its own awakening. And that universal being is a different dimension of who we are, but rest assured, we are already that now.

We have access to both dimensions of who we are, but our awareness is habitually fixated on the small self-concept point of view. For the past few hundred years, establishing a self-concept was a primary focus in human development, but at this point, with the self-concept so firmly in place, it seems that a fruitful direction for spiritual growth is toward greater recognition of our universal being.

Initially, our habit of identifying with the small self-identity will cause us to interpret our experiences of greater Self-awareness as us waking up to universal aspects of our true nature. But from another, equally valid, point of view, a universal being is waking up to its true nature through the vehicle of our self-identity.

Spiritual growth is the growth of the Self-awareness of the universe and us at the same time. I believe this is what is meant in the Hindu tradition when the great saints proclaim that Atman (individual being) and Brahman (universal being) are one.

We participate in the process of spiritual growth when we consciously and deliberately allow the awakening process of universal being to occur through us. To do this, we must awaken to the movement of universal being in our own experience and then surrender ourselves to the momentum of it like a surfer on a big wave. In other words, we must enter a flow state with life's process of spiritual awakening and growth.

When we give ourselves to the currents of universal being, we are swept up by a profound source of energy into higher and higher dimensions of reality. Assumptions of separation and isolation fall away like the skin of a snake as we expand into the fullness of who we really are.

But this is only the beginning, because the fullness of who we really are is becoming fuller all the time. There is always more and more to awaken to. The universal being is ever-expanding. I am describing two dimensions of an awakening process. One in which we awaken into the fullness of universal being and another in which we discover that we are a universal being awakening into higher and higher dimensions of its Self.

Once we have personally woken up to the universal aspect of our being, we have the opportunity to consciously participate in the further awakening of that being.

The challenge we face is that our consciousness is rigidly shaped by conditioned habits that belong to a paradigm built to support the experience of being a separate isolated individual. Our experience is filtered by that paradigm so that reality only shows up for us through a lens formed by the assumption of our separate existence.

Our perceptions are filtered, sorted, arranged, and categorized according to mechanisms of mind that themselves lie hidden in deep recesses of our unconscious. A huge amount of mental effort is being made behind the scenes to make sure that our picture of reality is consistent with the way we've been conditioned to believe the world works.

Any evidence that would challenge our preconceptions about reality is most often unconsciously dismissed so that it is never seen. Occasionally, a piece of incongruent information gets through the dominant paradigm's defenses. We experience something that shouldn't be possible.

For many of us, these anomalies of perception spur a spiritual search because they poke a big hole in our assumptions about what is true and who we are. Once the façade of our perceived reality has been punctured, some of us find it very difficult to return quietly to the way things were.

We now realize that there is more to reality, maybe much more than what we have ever seen before. We realize that we are not who we think we are, reality is much bigger than what we have been told, and so much more is possible than we ever imagined. I would call this recognition a spiritual awakening and those who have had one, large or small, have discovered the entryway to a life of participation in the universal process of awakening.

After an awakening, we become transitional beings. We stand in the doorway with one foot on both sides of a threshold, ready to act as a bridge between the universal consciousness and the manifest reality of the familiar world.

From this place, we can reach into the possibilities of a wider being and allow them to enter into the world through acts of profound creativity. To do this, we must enter a very special space in consciousness, a space that abides between our ordinary paradigm-delineated awareness and the unbounded receptivity of what is often called non-dual consciousness.

This is the space of between-ness. It is a space of magic and mystery. In this space, you are neither here nor there, now nor then, awake nor asleep. Realizing the creative potential of this magical space depends on being highly directed and utterly free at the same time. We must be single-mindedly focused and, at the same time, absolutely unattached to outcome. If we are, then we enter a dream-like state where it becomes possible to surrender our energy to support the emergence of a higher way of being, a meta-being.

I enter into this space particularly when I write,

paint, or teach. I let go of the world as it is and allow the boundaries and dividing lines that define reality to soften. Everything begins to bleed into everything else. The separation between you and me, this and that, now and then, here and there, all become blurry. The light of higher possibilities begins to shine through the edges of everything, illuminating forces from beyond the bounds of my awareness that begin to move me with unfamiliar emotions, insights, and intuitions. When we open into the mystery of being and give up control, while at the same time engaging in the process of creation, we can participate in the emergence of a meta-being through the growth of our higher Self-awareness. This is what I see as the most profound value of flow states and the ultimate purpose of spiritual life.

Flow tends to be the psychic signature of world-class performance and paradigm-shifting breakthroughs.

~ STEVEN KOTLER

Selected Bibliography

Belgrad, Daniel. *The Culture of Spontaneity: Improvisation and the Arts in Postwar America*. University of Chicago Press, 1999.

Csikszentmihalyi, Mihaly. *Flow: The Psychology of Optimal Experience*. Harper Perennial Modern Classics, 1990.

Kotler, Steven. *The Rise of Superman: Decoding the Science of Ultimate Human Performance*. Amazon Publishing, 2014.

Maclean, Norman. *Young Men and Fire*. University of Chicago Press, 1992.

Slingerland, Edward. *Trying Not to Try: The Art and Science of Spontaneity*. Crown, 2014.

Whitehead, Alfred North. *Adventures of Ideas*. Simon & Schuster Inc., 1933.

About the Author

Jeff Carreira is a meditation teacher, mystical philosopher and author who teaches to a growing number of people throughout the world. As a teacher, Jeff offers retreats and courses guiding individuals in a form of meditation he refers to as The Art of Conscious Contentment. Through this simple and effective meditation technique, Jeff has led thousands of people in the journey beyond the confines of fear and self-concern into the expansive liberated awareness that is our true home.

Ultimately, Jeff is interested in defining a new way of being in the world that will move us from our current paradigm of separation and isolation into an emerging paradigm of unity and wholeness. He is exploring some of the most revolutionary ideas and systems of thought in the domains of spirituality, consciousness, and human development. He teaches people how to question their own experience so deeply that previously held assumptions about the nature of reality fall away to create space for dramatic shifts in understanding.

Jeff is passionate about philosophy because he is passionate about the power of ideas to shape how we perceive reality and how we live together. His enthusiasm for learning is infectious, and he enjoys addressing student groups and inspiring them to develop their own powers of inquiry. He has taught students at colleges and universities throughout the world.

Jeff is the author of numerous books including:

The Art of Conscious Contentment, *No Place But Home*, *The Miracle of Meditation*, *The Practice of No Problem*, *Embrace All That You Are*, *Philosophy Is Not a Luxury*, *Radical Inclusivity*, *The Soul of a New Self*, and *Paradigm Shifting*.

For more about Jeff or to book him for a speaking engagement, visit: jeffcarreira.com

Made in United States
Orlando, FL
19 May 2024

47032192R00055